THE SECRET LIVES OF PUNCTUATIONS, VOL. I

THE SECRET LIVES OF PUNCTUATIONS, VOL. I

For Alex

Eileen R. Tabios

xPress(ed) * Espoo * 2006

ISBN 952-99702-0-X

Cover Image: "Conway" (1995) by Eve Aschheim. Oil,
charcoal, graphite on canvas. 14 x 11 in. Courtesy of
Galatea Art Collection, St. Helena, CA.
Photo by Thomas Pollock.

Design by Jukka-Pekka Kervinen

xPress(ed)
Tatartie 3 A 4
02620 Espoo
Finland
info@xpressed.org
www.xpressed.org

CONTENTS

I

; SONG IS SUBJECTIVE

"In the rounded olive screen of a very old television set, she looked at her own distorted image and turned away from it toward the window. Through the cloudy pane, she saw the top of a blooming peony bush."
—*from* **The Enchantment of Lily Dahl**
by Siri Hustvedt

; TO STUDY ART IS TO BECOME THIN

; despite Cezanne's desire, the world is never unclad

; to peruse a painting (intently) and see only one's
uncertainty over where to look

; mistaking science for "bathroom graffiti"

; why flinch when penetration results from the swish of
a kilt

; figuration, not abstraction, the synonym for ambiguity

; white velvet ribbon become bookmark

; lace

; CLOUDS EFFECT

; anything as a self-portrait

; why we persist in ignoring the inherent illusions in
Ph.D. theses revolving around "turns-of-the-century"

; confused as to whether lashes detract or enhance eyes
formed from pale blue sapphires

; to behave by doing favors is to engender regret

; the significance of clouds perpetually capped by satin
cobalt

; tears never dilute the color of a gaze

; mercury

; THE LOSS OF A WOOL COAT

; the unknown source of the pause

; to freeze the spiral that is memory's perspective

; open window, Bach ... *faintly*

; someone's marrow melts into soup

; revolt of a minor key

; pepper the visual substitute for truffles

; exodus

; THE HIDDEN LOGIC OF BIRTHS NECESSITATING VIOLENCE

; retrieving that thought I didn't know was missing

; "I liked to have Daddy's eyes on me"

; the lavender hue of anticipation hovering over the crowd preparing a communal evening meal

; carrots sliced into unsatisfying translucence

; the mother snapped the umbilical cord with her teeth, strapped the newborn to her back, then picked up the scythe

; near the end, the eyes take on an ascetic's bright, ecstatic gleam

; wings

; A TENDERNESS SO PAINFUL

; asleep, she beheld him then

; to discover perimeter by where your lips land

; personifying the impenetrability of knitting

; a child the remnant of a fading illusion

; a bed for slicing oceans

; the purse pulsing from persimmons

; persimmon

; WRITING PAST MARGIN

; but all side streets point to wrong directions

; violence via the infant shreaking

; nothing behind a corner, really

; seduction as wet cobblestones

; scent of a lunatic negative

; a god envying decay

; math

; THE SECOND LAST CHANCE

; rough skin a map

; allowing entry for what a lover represents

; the glue of ifs

; on edge through a silver lash

; overhearing the language shared by a toddler and a stuffed animal

; unfurling an antique wedding veil

; bone

; THE POSSIBLE GLOW

; the most effective beast must lack compulsion

; how blue becomes golden in a Cimabue

; waiting out the ash in one's mouth until morning

; then, part the curtain to face the well

; to complete paintings by allowing viewers' shadows

; reproduce half-tones from a photograph

; ember

; ONLY INCHES

; then see so much the brain implodes

; what makes a language move left to right on a page

; painting cracks

; to break routine by replacing apple with carrot

; I substituted my face with wings

; respond to mysteries with a kiss

; frightening

; ROMANTICIZING TUBERCULOSIS

; suspended on the scent of a violet

; his hands always released the thoughts they grabbed

; "O, what crusade is this?"

; slack with spent pleasure

; a room bereft of piano lessons

; o, the destructive ways of goodness

; dwarf

; HOPE FOR ENCHANTMENT

; the redhead during Verdi

; solitary breakfasts persisting to form such a long row

; rain, then a dangerous happiness

; her gown extends her skin

; you bookstopping a row of muddied dreams

; clarity—the wake of a bold breeze

; bells

; *THE EMBODIMENT OF LANGUAGE*

; the impossibility of bottoming out

; a hug pricked by small, slanted bones

; naked, due to intrusion by a bruise

; softened by the presence of hair

; "these were borrowed gestures"

; the names of children not born, like *Alexander*

; pearls

; AT BEST, A LIFTED CHIN

; a dropped sausage returned to a customer's plate

; leached of passion until reading material becomes
anything but novels

; cry, because the air is *felt*

; the sacrilege of orange eyelashes

; a speech written in response to a childhood slight

; sausage fat sizzles

; molasses

; *UNPLAYED PIANO MUSIC*

; bites the cheek to release blood when she utters "blood"

; stillness of the barn, moss rising between slate tiles

; where were you when it happened

; over the hill, a choir

; spilled tea

; apples rotting on lawn

; *Salieri*

; THE BACK OF A NAPKIN

; which one story to retain?

; the wine not as sweet as the offer

; she softens through sleep

; I began to know at age 43

; the willed decision obviating "mistake"

; ice relaxing its contours into liquid gold

; 645-1133

; THE COLLAPSE OF THE LAST LOG

; to find a house that can hold you and know what's in my bones

; becoming Beauty through anguish

; the logic of preferring books for maintaining passion ~~in their sights~~

; to lighten his load by not looking into his eyes

; the sunray sears the stallion

; a car fender sears her thigh

; implode

; THE UNRAVELING STITCH

; feeling the falsity of a book's last page

; then, intimacy as a glistening patch of skin

; money as measurement

; the pathos of the word "ethos"

; words read through a mirror

; seams caused by bindings

; paste

; THE PALPABILITY OF TWIN YOLKS

; when the stutter steadied itself

; such distance between "bell close" and "bellicose"

; was the red a welt or a velvet chair

; I am chasing the nude—make that, *gloriously naked!*—author

; I am writing not reading a book

; the shutter steadies itself

; eggs

; ~~FUSSY~~ KNICK-KNACKS

; to paint deeply into the night to wake up to something
untouchable

; feeling cheated at overhearing one is a source of
happiness

; ordinary, but still anguished

; the whiteness of the white mug

; explain light through algebra

; timid dust

; fringe

; THIN MUSIC

; her ~~feathers~~ snow tucked away amid silk negligees

; a face, nameless in a bookstore

; twin knotholes

; browning edge of lace forming narrative for "ancient"

; film of yellow dust

; a wave of grasshoppers blocking the view

; heifer

; HALF-BREED SIAMESE

; that pinched cheek

; meager pity

; pictures that can be nailed only against mental walls

; the lost joker card

; "one of an old man's peculiarities"

; metal chocolate

; mulish

; EX-GARTER

; one fat fading peony blossom crushed against the windowpane

; the fallible blues

; it flies towards a junk heap

; rouged nipples

; lace formed by fine wrinkles

; oily handshake

; noiseless

; NO MUSIC IN HIS VOICE

; when accomplishing a portrait ends the relationship

; delusion as a threshold into intimacy

; black sun formed via red rim

; omission as confession

; a blue wooden egg amidst white real eggs in yellow bowl

; "moonlight shone as hundreds of broken pieces on the moving water" (P. 215)

; convulse

II

.

THE ESTRUS GAZE(S)

"Our affinity would meet in being filled with archaic darkness and persisting memories of a time when all things were one, even in the midst of individual responsibility."
—*from* **Songs of a Gorilla Nation: My Journey Through Autism** *by Dawn Prince-Hughes*

: CONTEXT AND STRAWBERRIES

: when ripeness becomes "unfinished" if the matured object refuses to be eaten

: the insistence that glass shifts because of a "pretty illusion" articulated as "ancient sea"

: some poems, yes, should be silent when lifted from the page

: a zoo with non-existent cages

: the gorilla's fingerprint forms the outline of your face

: ceasing the hurtle through cold, dark Milky Way

: relax...*ation*

: ARCHAEOLOGY

: "You were standing by the gate of a zoo"

: to turn time into eternity, as gorillas do, by making it about presence not absence

: *Oh! That hot lemon smell of gorillas, and the thicksweet smell of the hay!*

: we are all born

: the haven defined as "utter lack of inspection"

: God as Love without a steeple for there has never been a roof

: smorgasbord

: HAYSTACK

: salt from expired matchheads

: background defined as the melting colors from a
spinning globe

: unfamiliarity with the edges of one's body

: a meltdown if the evening ends without exactly seven
lightning bugs in a jar

: this flawed archaeology when conducted fearfully!

: "heaven" defined as "a place where nothing changes"

: pebbles

: WILD

: the all-consuming business of prehistoric histrionics

: refusing to believe math is synonymous with description

: place become person

: sodden tissue balled up into a small, dead bird

: fleshing out the ghosts of unicorns

: a complexion formed from miles and miles of bad and bad roads

: "dreadlocks"

: THE ESTRUS GAZE

: heal face blindness by introducing — acknowledging —
context

: incomplete narratives formed from remnants not yet
borne away by birds, tiny animals, *wind*

: inevitably, egg yolks fragmenting from a table's edge

: we make love to concede to nostalgia

: the wave is perfect for being temporary, though not
conceded by surfers apostrophed by snow flakes
coagulating into white ponytails

: relief introduced by words forming a consistent, never-
ending pattern

: holograph

from
THE MASVIKIRU QUATRAINS

*"I take the dead out of the stone and find the
sculpture."*
—Lazarus Takawira, Shona sculptor

*"When one looks at great Shona sculpture—its
powerful mass, sharp edges, delicate balance, straight
masterful lines -- the technical mastery of the one
who carved it is obvious. Admiration turns to
incredulity and awe when one realizes the context in
which it was carved Despite the incredible
proportion and balance many artists achieve, there is
no pre-sketching, pre-drafting, or pre-shaping of their
work. It issues from deep in their mind's eye. Many
of these carvers, working outside their rural imbas,
simply sit in the dirt and begin with a crude tool in
their hands and a vision in their head."*
—*from* **Spirits in Stone: Zimbabwe Shona
Sculpture** *by Anthony and Laura Ponter*

THE FOURTH PAGE

foolery: pollinate eyrie
progress: retinal runners-up
forger: nimbus dowdy
round-the-clock: penetrate rot

proton: airship lire
Vaseline: nose dive
freebie: damper promiscuous
specialize: betterment bloat

persuasiveness: midget manipulative
IQ: crabbed Ra
spage-age: hula slake
faintness: instrument snowsuit

lachrymal: slickness profuse
AM: ahem misfire
idiomatic: rations periscope
thrash: quarry inhalator

hobbyist: converse sheaves
epoxy: semen discrepancy
trillion: planetary wintergreen
anthem: lumber jealousy

lodge: slippery atty.
campanile: softball issuance
liquefy: pox downwards
averse: amicable perquisite

copra: nameless feasibility
panorama: negotiable dorm
decadence: outflank tweedy
offal: conjoin uncounted

plainclothesman: radicalism dire
skin: N.Mex. woodwind
upstart; gravestone outmaneuver
pointy: Mediterranean fend

THE FIFTH PAGE

referendum: resell insipid
armed: reproach forbidden
wave: entrapment parallelism
twinkle: unsold reusable

mudslide: sewing white
whereby: compendium gable
pinkish: anthropoid coastal
talent: scout interruption

allot: midterm housework
alternator: northeast kettle
Congress: defensive mordant
bullet: squeaky obedient

slander: squirrel playwright
parsnip: attribute corn
defilement: spaciousness multitude
segment: southernmost participant

radiance: anarchy eyelid
amity: insurance nowadays
presumptuous: causation woodland
bombastic: spherical bounteous

neuralgia: oldie hallelujah
cyanide: effect pompadour
Kleenex: squeamish strife
expurgation: crawler saleable

urban: illiberal vapidity
catastrophic: charger milieu
sardine: opposite jigsaw
philistine: Grecian oven

scant: aura deploy
rudder: busy dashiki
wolverine: brushwood desecration
promoter: romance teem

THE SIXTH PAGE

ensemble: keypunch gimpy
precedence: dessicate endear
nosy: academy center
apotheosis: teaspoon secede

presupposition: windjammer urea
tailgate: void commandment
dejection: look masturbation
streetlight: dialogue spank

millennia: tanker extortion
thrall: cleanser denouement
disentanglement: ne'er-do-well fixate
geopolitics: par approbation

unpronounceable: factionalism buttress
bread: unmentionable Roman
market: unstudied Senator
loiterer: destroyer indoors

malnourished: reptile bedroom
cavalry: aromatic prosaic
tadpole: venison yeast
descendant: prude confine

bald: eagle tub
schmaltz: trailer blvd.
thicken: defecate immigrate
rejuvenation: frugality importune

biathlon: distillery ultrasonic
Apache: open-air superhighway
harridan: around-the-clock skullduggery
censure: repentant rump

disparagement: sylvan psoriasis
umlaut: constituent M
singularity: downwards truss
novelette: aviary principality

THE SEVENTH PAGE

scandalize: ulcer janitor
junior: pharmaceutical pogrom
guilder: syndication disposition
chrysalis: starlet amid

perky: celibacy air
gambit: offal banana
impugn: shirt trachea
compliance: armored willowy

heartbreak: sotte voce semantic
turboprop: industrial controllable
penance: indices algorithm
transfusion: kingdom voucher

cynic: enumeration monkey
tedium: spleen weep
stateliness: sparseness iridescence
backslider: exult backwater

opera: transmutation mooch
squirrel: scrunch denouement
hornless: inglorious bulkhead
optimist: piper remaining

ornamental: carton dilute
a la mode: debatable defense
biotechnology: godson loneliness
zirconium: carburetor crudeness

touchdown: dwarves hurtful
Muhammad: engraver troupe
pantomime: bestridden proscenium
succulence: pro circumcise

scrambler: unstuck pulchritude
kleptomaniac: salary manifesto
napalm: courtship attune
smudgy: job give

THE EIGHTH PAGE

supreme: dyestuff displace
abrasion: ostentation self-esteem
shipbuilder: thruway cunnilingus
toenail: perambulate bullish

tentacle: sergeant haddock
chlorophyll: apiary optional
powwow: coed volume
commandments: scriptwriter hormonal

misapprehension: thoughtless zippy
puny: unity stink
photocopier: extremity French
sapsucker: riff quintuple

secretariat: bragger snowmobile
decompress: throughway OPEC
professor: minutia civil
wonderment: incisive mother-of-pearl

hew: windsock supplant
engineering: rebate euphoria
neurological: role double-dealing
neophyte: epicure gig

defoliation: modicum begin
domain: better disinfectant
majestic: occupy intestine
derringer: bedeck collage

repose: straightness walrus
fungi: percolate heredity
poultry: wraparound flapper
EKG: persevere indiscriminate

oxide: stripling game
parvenu: Lutheran underwritten
tubercular: strapless euphemism
patriarchy: lax chatter

THE NINTH PAGE

pavilion: heron vis-à-vis
neurotic: ACLU twill
eczema: windshield promoter
seabed: virility monotheism

lassie: wayfaring stepsister
mastermind: keynote whitener
photon: notion upstart
cynical: aerospace GNP

appointment: delicatessen antacid
tepee: modem grueling
casserole: Cajun intrusion
winery: tend globular

sermon: hidebound waddle
fortnight: innate fling
consulate: verity covetous
unswerving: truck dragon

otter: livable champagne
carbine: surprising propane
photocopy: mucus Filipino
dictum: slip-up innate

dollhouse: sunspot repress
cruciform: diastolic green
brunette: sitcom tablet
cease-fire: slope heroine

osteopathy: laudatory pj's
alphanumeric: ersatz affinity
anchorman: variety convene
mercantile: chivalrous university

parachute: shamrock rebuke
miscellany: expedite spatter
workhorse: cadmium themselves
genocide: honoraria brain-dead

THE TENTH PAGE

monarchic: cross-examination matte
research: blindness Semitic
goad: encrustation distort
delinquency: tutorial causeway

passerby: wishy-washy archer
morpheme: panoramic punk
enormity: Gypsy blintz
arborvitae: descend nonstop

halves: clomp euphemistic
excavator: nursemaid brew
propulsion: unsanitary dictionary
doggedness: bean fierce

convex: Arthur oviparous
delirium: teenager hereditary
herbicide: acronym implicit
triangle: lucrative remonstrance

bedfellow: overpower cogitate
construe: cuspid ratty
adrenal: proprietress saltcellar
munificence: comptroller turnkey

purl: anonymity running
peevish: reprehend reverberate
washable: porch limit
peseta: continental trowel

buttermilk: warhorse solicitation
magistrate: kickstand crater
mussel: thespian drawbridge
browbeat: disembarkation pygmy

Messiah: heehaw chauvinism
Islamic: diameter categorize
Goldfinch: celluloid plaster
Paris: mallet bemoan

maternity: comforting embroider
rosette: demagnetize equation
verdigris: damask broth
pendulum: fraternal freedom

gravitational: unique margarine
polecat: hairdressing retrospection
unassuming: avarice Iron
inauspicious: slough toenail

metabolic: lightness catalpa
Viking: pea perceptible
lambaste: desiderata loony
tombstone: hardheadedness eligibility

evacuee: operator sassafras
gulag: floppy mandatory
alphabetic: execution FM
cogency: improvise bigamist

testate: music puck
perpetuation: countable wind
mangrove: February flay
excrete: soundtrack blight

mousse: concavity maunder
paleontology: demolish neatness
asymmetrical: putrid translucence
abstemious: applicant saxophonist

feathery: thesaurus dodo
Eustachian: hula pedigreed
buffoonery: Burgundy syncopate
maritime: anticlimactic tie

colloquium: facilitate senna
manna: sweeping sulphur
profligate: pilothouse mother-in-law
sweetener: crisis elevation

THE TWELFTH PAGE

tibia: decomposition zodiac
consular: pestle weather
godless: nonevent jeans
impeccable: exclamation bract

savvy: mutability obstacle
notify: cosmetology antitheses
repletion: sled oleander
fluid: crotch fjord

stripling: spring enticement
tenderness: daydream technician
deflation: prevaricator stub
deflation: jack adjutant

waggish: sonar once-over
crucify: slip-up yokel
octogenarian: livable bubble
weevil: fib limerick

dentistry: exclamatory awful
crocodile: epileptic uncharitable
Filipino: conviction encyclopedic
relocation: dependency series

thunderbolt: infringe eager
cockatoo: spacey mandible
cowpox: arson sophisticate
trippery: triumvirate gunnery

ménage: dissolution suspenseful
disputatious: imperialist homer
xenophobic: etiquette clandestine
wing: willies lucid

beryllium: quick mayonnaise
vocal: corpus lame
transact: garble episodic
hedonistic: patchy gamin

THE THIRTEENTH PAGE

equine: elbow libelous
julep: enslave flu
hackney: width puncture
spiritualistic: effluent grim

alliteration: tubercular obstruct
tartar: periphery cystic
opprobrium: wallaby handcart
lavish: tripe oviparous

jewel: precipitate trenchant
severe: driftwood plastic
donut: campy impart
turpitude: lung bureaucratic

rotisserie: feta deceitfulness
maiden: pate pep
impalpable: uninvited urbane
encrustation: stair vegan

comprehensible: abnegation exposition
unprovoked: irony sheepish
muckrake: conch trimester
factotum: unhealthy hereabout

auxiliary: Lutheran corpuscle
unanimity: splat oakum
demagogy: hazard ginger
logistic: porno doxology

pauperism: owlish symptom
mulatto: wineglass emphysema
concrete: argue requisite
ulna: weary median

chattiness: excreta Freudian
simile: ingénue betrayal
imp: blunderbuss anon.
hairdo: numerate letdown

THE FOURTEENTH PAGE

hard-on: controllable patrol
mendicant: reverential captive
homogenize: microchip sanity
dishwasher: limited pedicure

elephantine: wobble cannonade
mellifluous: unbearable outcast
osteopath: promotional flange
mire: musky global

hoedown: renter X
chromosome: trapezoid head-on
barricade: predilection biochemistry
luster: skunk Scotsman

Angolan: spiteful laser
commodore: anthill enthusiastic
archduke: conferment longitude
ointment: public periodontal

lime: strove concubine
optima: cutback outré
gazebo: recollection robustness
bluegrass: flame paranoia

queue: prompter outward
ventriloquism: loincloth wry
parsimony: excess speed
limit: monetary coitus

dehumanize: Grecian apprentice
youngish: unrequited montage
groggy: indolent noblesse
disengagement: mar FAA

emery; influential cohabit
stupor: syrup matchmaker
jawbreaker: clover intolerance
adapter: perusal beg

THE FIFTEENTH PAGE

cancer: anniversary tanker
burnt: manners obsolescent
ND: egregious cross
singe: uvula implore

accouterments: myriad aria
trellis: gulf commissioned
creosote: enumerate wax
bulimia: base wizardry

bitumen: submarine dressmaking
nary: biped ubiquity
traduce: henpecked plaque
immune: prize isolation

forgettable: goalkeeper refinish
screwdriver: advantage shield
enthusiast: portmanteau headset
well-meaning: loaded sports

proximity: wend unsportsmanlike
undemanding: nematode forced
pinochle: histrionic handout
entente: concede theorem

antisocial: rhetorical per
precipitous: stillbirth earthwork
participle: Mongoloid oops
groundhog: adjunct sourness

kidnapper: ethic goulash
earthiness: desolate staph
rearview: helmet pose
judiciary: piquancy bow

ingratiating: comedy trendy
fender: entourage recessional
inadvertence: cedilla gift
enervate: postage rundown

THE SIXTEENTH PAGE

pantomime: agnosticism disclosure
ascent: thereabout wringer
aforesaid: delivery recourse
barbarism: decrepitude blood

carnage: thunderclap cantankerousness
speedometer: beneficial skittish
horticulture: insubstantial TN
diaphanous: trench Neptune

hedonist: oldie watering
repercussion: inveigle bogeyman
bunkhouse: slaver bloodcurdling
safari: start insurrection

tedium: large-scale courtesan
transgressor: tipster port
frowzy: background anagram
velours: arithmetic pathogen

tolerable: obstetric deep
magnanimity: glean Chinese
finicky: curdle curie
pituitary: sewage uncooperative

zestful: perdition African-American
phantasy: unused sunny
sonorous: crisp hookworm
placentae: windswept plankton

intricacy: triplicate hormone
Aries: runner-up teacher
leguminous: aggressiveness torture
interpreter: squaw priestess

cello: gurney hoaxer
overanxious: felony crony
cupboard: blotting paper
sacramental: god-awful exhort

THE SEVENTEENTH PAGE

bodkin: moonshine petticoat
Mother: unimaginable pellmell
frequency: antiknock repertory
peeling: compilation opium

heedless: euphoria flat
denigrate: squint moldiness
baleful: dreary syphilitic
defecation: finery hogshead

ulceration: antiwar chafe
musket: ivy parabola
enormity: glacial role-playing
shrink-wrap: diffusion sawdust

liposuction: blithe insider
CB: frizzy grad
tenderloin: forsythia nobleness
governor: germanium ironing

conscript: tumble preferential
lapidary: ecumenical betrothal
dispatcher: excision brilliant
tendonitis: horseback earth

fortification: fatuous waltz
warmed-over: haven't full-blooded
simulator: slaphappy harelip
llama: unceremonious tangible

military: medicate defiance
fencing: foreseen denture
plasticity: morgue impulse
blasphemer: gland unkindness

inaudible: manliness cosmetology
emasculate: protractor Midwestern
microorganism: contemptible purr
abdicate: ill-starred menopause

THE EIGHTEENTH PAGE

legatee: screwball fifteenth
gymnasia: saunter indictable
womanizer: preconceived fire
wheedle: vagary slow-witted

suffragette: slain mineral
bosun: stagflation hazelnut
acrobat: clip joint
premiere: flagpole cocker

battery: sundae electrical
legalese: colonel seven
sanguine: Laotian streptococcus
evergreen: cyclic terry

desideratum: kiss orthodontist
checkerboard: inkwell forswore
quixotic: logical intuitive
griffin: shrill herbivore

gumdrop: jack-o-lantern upbringing
conjugal: intravenous myth
nebulae: gaudiness veer
portcullis: marsupial economist

klutz: heron solar
seashore: gentry jangle
audit: worm apron
slenderness: disabuse conjurer

antiparticle: exhumation transplantation
masseur: warty Congress
superscript: Flemish bleeder
archenemy: age swizzle

denature: flatter ligature
antebellum: lure rim
demobilization: topmost windjammer
marsupial: ovarian transpire

THE NINETEENTH PAGE

amatory: snafu productivity
esophagus: day semaphore
tuition: seismic fullback
urinary: U-boat croup

cockfight: steamship October
cusp: sober seedy
birdseed: transubstantiation mien
arithmetic: trench inadequacy

tumble: pi wow
Madonna: dishrag tote
Taiwanese: v mattock
grueling: specie athlete

erstwhile: divider p.m.
pitchfork: resin dressage
polar: mangrove accomplished
espousal: métier incompatible

marinate: ginkgo Miss
invective: deathlike savoir
revolver: skylark publish
seminary: twitter constabulary

pelvic: credentials nasturtium
galleon: obduracy aborigine
syllabify: boll artlessness
misjudgment: salsa spine

acoustic: sufficiency peripatetic
mascara: barium cop-out
octagon: heirloom pickings
miniskirt: G improvisation

Pyrex: infantile extrapolate
percale: morale fulminate
crevasse: roebuck bassist
Inferno: strange preconceive

THE TWENTIETH PAGE

thespian: desiccation trance
travail: vector deceit
peahen: Montessori benefaction
chop: ambivalent dissension

wanderlust: hill synod
republican: ambiguous trillionth
munchies: ballroom sickle
quadrille: cortical lira

suffix: validation herewith
loganberry: forage gibberish
accord: occidental crouton
annoyance: fishing leotard

elaborate: misread elaborate
confederate: painstaking turbulent
knockwurst: boundless subservience
bellows: battleship O

shrine: neutrino locus
incongruous: watchmaker unflappable
disfavor: shat stroke
streamer: paramedic predecease

surpass: constituency mulch
rpm: gory grease
U-boat: journeyman gunwale
ballot: projectile tamarind

missal: sniper Indian
liverwurst: remiss clasp
wool: homogeneity brainstorming
remove: slip brass

trifle: estimable time
pilferer: stereophonic twister
melon: unwieldiness medicinal
interpretive: valve megahertz

THE TWENTY-FIRST PAGE

disparaging: colicky buck
scooter: lit propagate
haziness: superimpose backhoe
stringer: legitimacy expressiveness

mastectomy: dulcimer solace
turbulent: fleur-de-lis gob
sapience: hear machine
differential: jeep dressing

computerization: retarded sash
unsteadiness: line scythe
functionary: southwest glumness
elder: statesman object

preoccupy: emirate bifocal
magnifier: bogy no-no
didactic: Capt. etymology
soothing: point coot

voltage: tribesman living
whisk: gourmand onion
chow: glint southerner
win: glisten landing

hang: quasar harry
combustible: nonprofessional beau
sensitive: compulsory red
Richter: inculcation unergo

surliness: insomnia station
PC: lull enroll
surname: exhibition trailblazer
lurch: ingredient RFD

consternation: Wyoming cleaver
arroyo: pixel thiamine
lifeblood: tabulate dowel
immoral: pastern palatial

THE TWENTY-SECOND PAGE

enviable: ungovernable deadliness
pollen: valve consequent
epitome: desecrate junkie
vernacular: entrance heavy

incestuous: Gaelic doddering
violinist: arpeggio chambermaid
moonstruck: vouch unabashed
irrefutable: unrelieved gallery

union: tendency heat
caffeine: serendipitous collocate
herewith: whoa typhoid
preciousness: supposing vestment

fatherland: considerate proof
aides-de-camp: beck transceiver
KO: grimness pizza
pipsqueak: derogation uniformity

propane: tuba penguin
Pharaoh: markdown cranky
exclusion: marine ballet
fragile: unrecognizable specify

disembarkation: choppiness shrinkage
nourish: missile curve
beaux: snitch suggestion
crowd: gallantry jogger

encyclopedia: bedside blow
altitude: piratical restructure
castanet: dipthong inimical
rapport: doublet slander

brooch: ground sodium
minty: diffidence paddock
forbade: teat turncoat
singularity: brighten motivate

THE TWENTY-THIRD PAGE

mystical: sheeting fanatical
vegetate: fudge behold
overriden: opossum chairperson
aloofness: vegetable improvement

alight: feeler vignette
pressurization: quicken serrated
videocassette: troubadour regime
alms: ache October

Syrian: propulsive lisp
welder: dashing February
wicket: lifesaver hard-on
scull: wench easterner

perimeter: nose-dive bookkeeping
AT: sconce litmus
capitalist: maddening die-hard
convince: dampen haunch

over-the-counter: starlit history
oxygenate: hesitate migrate
centralization: dairy notorious
Bunsen: unbutton maize

incursion: smartness false
squeamish: cheese tad
megaphone: gossip ventricle
caboose: fiction prevalent

depilatory: chemical electorate
prevaricate: Inca gluttonous
erratic: afire plait
mourning: heist repetitious

R&D: sushi lifer
stomachache: hackle solar
haze: steed antisocial
antics: designer serous

THE TWENTY-FOURTH PAGE

fleetness: cryptographer consist
levitation: neatness misrepresentation
prime: fox existentialist
carbonated: presupposition dewlap

raunchy: disciple scuzzy
rajah: abaft imperishable
breech: abaci vice
seabed: funky limelight

keenness: puck guilder
grandiloquence: towhead drawbridge
glassy-eyed: eiderdown harangue
crinoline: numeral silk-screen

viscous: harlequin cardiovascular
verdant: prologue abaft
secretarial: primate Plexiglas
reroute: accidental esprit

lucre: stoical wantonness
fob: aphrodisiac enchanter
chlorofluorocarbon: locution peacetime
mead: coyote nakedness

rehearsal: bigoted farm
Wyo.: prohibitionist leonine
asperity: duo escrow
kohlrabi: judicious NE

bandana: amphibian benchmark
saguaro: citronella sadness
machismo: retiring karate
abyss: bullfight conduit

homestretch: migrate stillbirth
mangle: template surtax
lading; flatulent takeout
wizard: kinfolk kick-start

THE TWENTY-FIFTH PAGE

parvenu: special despair
snigger: a la carte slackness
omnipresence: vocalize augmentation
kennel: gasket flashy

prow: follow-the-leader distracted
goblet: Negro epochal
caliph: canniness harry
social: endear abashed

jocular: Dominican split-level
chidden: machinery pep
double-barreled: busybody cull
jaguar: snowmobile object

oboist: commodity inhibited
palmetto: detector ptomaine
malady: depository Velcro
anarchism: enchantress gypsy

chopsticks: miscue ejaculation
hubris: border longitudinal
benzene: barrette data
mercy: worry every

bruise: ruinous barrio
resplendent: sifter sentimental
foible: kilohertz restricted
Venus: overpass Camambert

Newt: cerebral curfew
Jackhammer: sexism pederasty
barehanded: fungal bigot
literati: unshakeable G

brigantine: grip dish
vertebra: pact cohabitation
orthography: electrocardiogram quoth
riche: fated bruin

THE TWENTY-SIXTH PAGE

premises: beaux overdue
cohesion: representative junkie
son-in-law: shorten retrospective
xerographic: web=footed lethal

nonfatal: liquor decant
lofty: gorilla untrue
defaulter: immutability hunk
eskimo: mollify organdy

pooch: whey pressurize
roil: apology Genesis
aggrandize: militate chamomile
solstice: medium-sized disorganization

Jeremiah: streamer surmountable
daydreamer: translucent paltry
champion: rosin moccasin
transmittal: dinghy rove

aqueous: interpretative autism
sarsaparilla: exclusion magnetic
unwound: horse despondent
puree: terror solo

conquistador: bridegroom elapse
alliterative: sedentary pro
forbade: boggy pitch-black
abbreviation: individualist tampon

creditor: whosoever bankrupt
oppressive: unisex undefeated
shakedown: bouncing gunk
picnicker: cell matador

equinoctial: copulation autumn
commoner: bonehead exhale
tissue: theocratic bath
iridium: oblique horology

THE TWENTY-SEVENTH PAGE

burnoose: robotic assessor
Thursday: sewage lug
woodbin: unlace hemispherical
largesse: Austrian flowery

furtherance: sweater derringer
sodium: tumbleweed galosh
misty: things rebus
unstuck: circle slaughterer

sprout: malcontent coarsen
grill: vertebrate ego
staves: lady moustache
proximity: diversification uninjured

accede: palindrome sackcloth
pontiff: hour unconsciousness
sty: introverted jerky
mottled: current fiendish

avant-garde: lager ruling
cinder: politicize maggot
superhighway: alchemy forty
maharanee: direction impeccable

tulle: sullen trainee
Zeus: beatify mare
barmaid: cesspool irrespective
dressing: delete simile

transplantation: heck telegraphic
latency: spanking peril
cheerlessness: fries method
populous: pittance Great

trapezoid: scrunch tongue
pump: exasperation dry
unseasoned: reprehensible yardarm
flagship: independence bereft

THE TWENTY-EIGHTH PAGE

recession: nonpolluting distrust
capsule: potboiler tenuous
deuce: reiteration parapet
pathological: sugarcane gouge

eighty: aegis nomad
postnatal: forefront ounce
syrup: act Hera
repairable: sunburn Company

cystic: immolate fumble
frog: arrant satirical
unwashed: Masonic appreciable
crackdown: competitiveness coffee

nevermore anguished temptress
cobalt: flatfish trickle
grindstone: rule backbreaking
glottis: serried monogram

tutu: pinochle alto
blacktop: discretion asymmetry
evangelistic: commandant cottonwood
swashbuckler: thrum groveler

emu: pixel loneliness
dawdler: succotash cryptic
bellicosity: restaurateur pool
hairy: out-of-the-way embroil

sensor: twit mark
usury: detraction scull
rupee: rink exhortation
paganism: peeper solar

continua: chargeable herbivore
premature: sparrow marshmallow
suppliant: wishful lassie
eggshell: wherever invent

THE TWENTY-NINTH PAGE

everyday: superficial abrogate
heartlessness: base X
chromosome: intent unmade
reenlist: self-righteousness sentimentalist

commit: rat christening
nil: hospice scourge
pasturage: misdoing mumbler
lechery: allied dissimulate

guideline: incorrectness hypocrite
siding: pasteboard flush
troposphere: NC churl
basalt: prelate nectarine

behemoth: mesa oddball
MS: loudness go-ahead
miserable: forebode rainy
red-hot: bearish pug

bark: afternoon vulgarism
demagoguery: stellar patronize
infringe: self-propelled advice
matriculation: sulfide monarchy

enliven: jeer clothier
shareholder: pager windmill
gerund: worshiper anoint
vagrant: gluttonous predestination

groggy: redheaded geriatrics
serfdom: bare transcendental
volcanic: exude offend
tartar: Roquefort unwilling

appertain: institutional rebirth
entente: plantation awoken
allowable: shot glare
unassailable: oh catching

THE THIRTIETH TO SIXTY-FIFTH PAGES (I)

signification: suggestive rostrum
precursor: extrapolate thermodynamics
portage: coat geometrical
water-repellent: Wednesday sometimes

scumbag: antidote deserve
breaststroke: adman unsafe
awry: slunk narcissist
cipher: fortuitous gout stalk

leafless: romantic foggy
vamoose: scullery kink
gluttonous: skinflint writ
ganglia: peeling CT

continental: expose reckless
reconnoiter: intermingle unmentionable
criterion: gild derriere
scuffle: typeset hankering

jackknife: superpower animosity
addressee: kernel behest
manpower: luster elite
nymphomania: kittenish veal

greenhouse: trapezoidal chemist
monument: disdain synopses
M.A.: loot tarpon
geographer: exorcism preponderant

elfin: hemp jounce
nourish: foremost touch
botanical: queen arcane
schmuck: vicar petrochemical

flatcar: anticlimactic unmade
gather: seaward aback
hanger: defuse soiree
dyspeptic: sword unconscionable

dipsomaniac: confidentiality alteration
outran: withholding tax
deadbolt: troops soapbox
tablespoonful: meantime figure

schizoid: mistress stylishness
ethnology: interest formalism
sewerage: cocktail sum
TV: apartheid iodine

backstop: patchy pea
leatherneck:" soliloquize overtax
raisin: puzzle gosh
soliloquy: watery MD

brunet: PO antimatter
lithograph: twelfth liberator
frankincense: patronize autocrat
patter: lb. cutlery

legerdemain: earnings rib
outbound: dermatology update
monotone: conservation torrid
rattlesnake: calcify inveterate

valuation: hanky-panky carbonation
incarcerate: facetious litre
emirate: twitter harelip
herbaceous: bistro seditious

albeit: delimit zenith
promontory: interj. Spaniard
tangelo: appointment spiciness
noninterference: undisputed misspend

maxim: dishrag cannonade
woebegone: daddy vanquish
antacid: shuteye atomic
irreconcilable: nix squaw

shepherdess: cotton overmuch
saccharin: imaginary disgust
quaintness: deposit swop
snare: withstand bone

knoll: adenoidal roughneck
mortgagor: covenant motor
overemphasize: mukluk maturity
planetaria: redundant enact

morning: postmodern Pekingese
recklessness: distinctive actualize
Huguenot: tore likeness
sardine: mica discordant

congruity: fiancé Frankenstein
diabetic: sawdust wire
gravel: dewdrop breakwater
stimulation: yeasty coronary

ambassadorial: nonsmoker mouthpiece
avocation: unpaid loyal
maraschino: demagoguery impulsiveness
bronco: matzo stool

blanch: floss spatula
phonetic: remarriage reminder
reflection: paraprofessional mezzo-soprano
bologna: fourteen gasohol

perpetuate: plumpness pretzel
escapist: glassware grandmother
unscientific: overpower pneumatic
catarrh: emblem nonviolent

salve: ruination iota
sinkhole: maul Bermuda
speculation: horseback educated
kamikaze: rainstorm schizoid

blue-collar: inconstant fumigate
coincidence: dessert affix
lampoon: vulture hydroponics
sangfroid: alluvial preposition

AZT: shy hirsute
blossom: poodle unfashionable
letter: paleness fiesta
isosceles: language bombshell

insemination: overdone capacitor
caldron: halcyon fool
egalitarianism: evening double
enthuse: immorality congress

thyroid: drift partiality
gopher: homograph kick-start
maharani: hypochondria jeweler
lath: participatory confused

insomniac: middle mare
organdie: chocolate cardinal
gross: wide-awake mousiness
tad: reversible cue

colonization: rhino gherkin
refrigerator: apology Messrs.
gentry: centrist punster
half-and-half: deposit copter

mignon: debris embark
generative: amoebae roughneck
eventide: celebrate trapezoidal
delicacy: cockfight jackknife

abstruse: torsion interwoven
ripple: leather sometimes
silica: reclamation protoplasm
oblivion: unreasoning laundress

tic: trumpet tubercle
obeisance: billow chick
househusband: silicosis howdy
bogeyman: burlesque gift

histrionics: roundness sardine
outsmart: meddler roommate
devil-may-care: wiliness connective
aster: stupefaction hut

antechamber: ocher untroubled
graciousness: meant conceptualize
insensibility: vertices parquet
lemonade: bestow phalanx

frown: majority mathematical
Navaho: wonder obtrude
homonym: tonsil carbon
dioxide: resources amateurism

A POETICS

AN EKPHRASIS: ON THE PATH OF THE SHONA TO SCULPT "THE MASVIKIRU QUATRAINS"

"In my poetry I do not try to find the words to express what I want
        to say.
In my poetry I try to find ways to express what the words have
        to say."
—*Carl Andre*

"Though these visions are influenced by ancestors, the sculpture is
not used in ritual or ceremony. In the West, most African art is
defined as consisting of either religious icons or practical artifacts,
meaning tools used in daily life. But this definition has been imposed
on Africa by outsiders and certainly does not fit Shona sculpture or
other contemporary African art forms. Shona sculpture is neither
worshipped nor functional. It is purely decorative—art for art's
sake."
—*from* **Spirits in Stone: Zimbabwe Shona Sculpture** *by*
Anthony *and* Laura Ponter

I wrote "The Masvikiru Quatrains" as a result of Jukka-Pekka Kervinen's poetry collection, *cornucopia* (xPress(ed), 2004). From Zimbabwe's Shona culture, "masvikiru" means "spirit mediums." But before I tell you about my poems, let me share some background about their inspiration.

Jukka wrote *cornucopia* as a sample of what he calls "statistical writing." Basically, the poem results from a computer program, in this case one that utilizes three statistical distributions—uniform, binomial, and Gaussian (normal)—to avoid patterns. The (pattern) exception is that, in punctuation, a period is used each time the program encounters a space in its source vocabulary. For *cornucopia*, Jukka's sources were excerpts from John Locke's "The Essay of Toleration" and Antonio Gramsci's "Letters from Prison."

I enjoy collaborating with Jukka partly because he takes, as a beginning point, a very different—nay, perhaps the opposite—tack from how I approach my poems. That is, he deliberately tries to be dispassionate whereas I, robustly believing in subjectivity, fling myself naked, hair matted and blood rushing into the poetry-writing. [Cough.]

Exemplifying what I mean about Jukka's approach is that, consistent with his long-time investigations into computer-generated texts and poems, Jukka says that he never edits the results: "My 'philosophy' is simple and clear: if I use the computer to generate music/poems I must be satisfied with the results without any editing. I don't change a single word/note. Otherwise I must do whole thing without computers!"

And yet the reason why *cornucopia* works as a poem is the strength of its poetic music—as soundscape—such that reading through it effortlessly allowed me to write new poems which I intended as pure (abstract) music. This leads me to the other reason why I like collaborating with Jukka: we may begin from disparate if not opposite points, but we end up in the same space for the poem: music.

cornucopia consists of 65 pages of words. There are no discernible beginnings or endings to the piece. There are no titles, line breaks or paragraph breaks. It's just a 65-page block of words. Yet, as I began reading it, I started reading music by sensing such music (through rhyme and rhythm and my subjective interpretations of pacing and tone) even as I also considered the text "visual" a la dark, seemingly single-color canvases.

After my read—and conclusion that what I experienced through such reading was music—I asked Jukka about his work. Jukka replied that he also found the computer-generated results "surprisingly musical." But as Jukka—who is also a composer—explained, "One reason for this might be that the program was first used to generate a cello piece (punctuation vs. silence/very loud (low) strokes)."

Jukka's referenced cello piece is available on the Internet at http://xpressed.sdf-eu.org/kervinen (see "Compositions-Computer-generated scores-eXudes for cello solo").

I hadn't intended to write poems as I read through *cornucopia*, but I found that each page offered a new poem. Specifically, each line on the page generated a three word line. For each line, the first word is followed by a colon so that the next two words offers a relationship to the first word based on said colon (I happened to be in the midst of investigating the colon punctuation mark when I began writing this series). Because the diction is based more on sound (music) vs. narrative meaning, I wanted to push the challenge of creating a colon-based relationship within each three-word line.

Reflecting the fact that each page of *cornucopia* contains 39 lines, the poems are formed from quatrains. Every fifth line on the page was deleted, with that line deletion becoming equivalent to a stanza break. Thus, each poem consists of eight quatrains, except for the last poem which is comprised of five quatrains as the last page contains only 24 lines.

To write—and hopefully for the reader to read—these

quatrains was/is an experience based on a sense of musicality in *cornucopia*. Moreover, *cornucopia* is so musical that even as I wrote my poems, I sensed that there were other parallel poems threaded through each of the pages. This may be made clearer by looking at the original *cornucopia* text for the first poem, "The Fourth Page" (shown in "Selected Notes to Poems"). In looking at the prose poem form of the source text, you might sense—as I do—that one could just as easily have formed different three-word combinations than what I chose for "The Masvikiru Quatrains." For instance, rather than the poem's version of the first quatrain

> foolery: pollinate eyrie
> progress: retinal runners-up
> forger: nimbus dowdy
> round-the-clock: penetrate rot

I could have written—chipped out from the stone-prose—the following for the first quatrain:

> notoriety: smirch resilience
> baptize: runners-up kilowatt
> impersonate: unceasing nimbus
> ménage: disingenuous moonscape

Another example is how the series' last poem, "The Thirtieth to the Sixty-Fifth Page," was created by stringing together the first quatrains from each of the referenced poems. For me, this implies that had this series' concern been only music, I also could have written the series' individual 66 poems as a single poem like Jukka's *cornucopia*, without page breaks or titles.

*****

78

However, I didn't write this series only from a sense of soundscape. Not only did I wish to extend my exploration of the colon punctuation mark, but I also wanted to translate Zimbabwean Shona sculpture methodology into writing poems. By the latter, I mean that I had to chip away at *cornucopia's* prose blocks to release new poems. Shona sculptors believe that (ancestral) spirits reside in stones and when they sculpt from stones, they basically are trying to release the spirits into what we later see as sculpted forms. From *cornucopia*, I sought to write poems to release the many hidden strains of music I sensed as spirits beneath each of *cornucopia's* pages.

As I learned about Shona sculpture, I also felt a kinship between the sculptors' approach and my long-time desire to write poems along the "first draft, last draft" vein. In *Spirits in Stone: Zimbabwe Shona Sculpture*, the authors Anthony and Laura Ponter describe the Shona sculpting process as:

> "The artists do not experience angst in the creative or carving process. When a sculpture does not emerge, it is simply cast aside. There is no regret. When a carving exploded during the firing process, destroying more than a month of work, artist Crispin June Mutambika said simply, 'It wasn't meant to be.' Shrugging off any disappointment, he picked up another stone and began anew." [126-127]

All of the poems in this book, including "The Masvikiru Quatrains," were written along the first draft, last draft mode. Nowadays, I attempt all of my poems in that manner. If a draft doesn't work, I don't file it (for further extensive or copious editing). I trash the "failed" first draft, believing that if there was some "spirit" (or poetic energy) sufficiently strong to generate a poem, it will come back to me and perhaps at that later date I will be more adept at guiding out its form in one (unedited) passage. I relate my way of writing to something the Ponters said: "Like most other acts in Shona culture, the carving is ... destined from its beginning."

To relate the poems further to Shona sculpture, one might say that Jukka and I have found as a common "ancestor" a type of music that draws out an empathy that we hold in common, a type of music that makes us kin. Through music, Jukka and I zero out notions of Other-hood. Through Poetry, we become the same flesh, blood ... and even computer.

THE COLON'S MIRROR: DOUBLE-COLONS

"one must be careful not to bestow / intention where
there may have been no more (much) than jostling //
possibility: keep jiggling the innumerable elements
and even integrations can fall out of disintegrations"
—from **Sphere: The Form of a Motion**
by A.R. Ammons

MY BAYBAYIN POEM
—*for Barbara J. Pulmano Reyes*

Oakland's cause : : outfielder finished off
       wants to be seen : : occasionally clucks
defensive adventures : : left-field gaps
       her sophisticated awareness : : "For they are
funny."

out of his glove : : run it down
       lingering resentment : : visiting Martian
rookie right : : a 2-2 pitch
       grand old dame : : context multiplicities

deciding blows : : victory over Orioles

"just came out" : : "no excuses"
       the network's grandees : : youth demographic
with the win : : four-game sweep
       too indecisive : : grow a beard

season high : : ahead of the Angels
       introducing Charlotte : : movie goes dry
ends tonight : : old advantage going
       veneer of sweets : : exploited slips

continue to play : : **jump-started, pump-started**
       grand ~~way of~~ walking : : over-analyzed appeal

October 30, 2005
—for Thomas Fink

the radiance we talk about : : fly swatted!
that part of the structureless lust : : dog panting
energy without frigging : : 'neath table a stalking cat

discontinuity imposed : : sneeze-roiled throat
opposing the normal intermingled sway : : dust mote
unmuddling of clarity : : ebb in water glass

cleansing invested with identity : :
                                        flooding New Orleans

III

( )

PARENTHETICALS

"(problem margin mad hymn optical slaying"
—from "obeyed dilemma" by Jukka-Pekka
Kervinen

(as if the number of
carats is symbolic)

(although the
audacity of the
cruelty was not his
primary **concern**)

(imagine **that** caravan
of hags)

(actually, can waves
be **gothic**?)

(expensive **bone**, that ivory)

(why wouldn't the sea **swallow** gold coins since they glint?)

(what is nullified
when butter **melts**)

(though it is the
hunted, coral **warns**)

(even **false** witches
can samba)

(she's always bullish
on the bogus, e.g.
"knight or monk, **or**
vice versa")

(cooks lacking
insurance!)

('twas the **first** time
she sewed for bit
maps)

(dungeons: a waste
of **marble**)

(regret a kingdom
with **unknown**
borders)

(she means, the
marrow of obliquity)

(forgiveness become
brass coin)

(snow **rents** the
night sky to
maximize the clarity
of a flood losing its
center)

(is it not impossible
for a decade to
weep?)

(oh, the
awkwardness **of**
trust!)

(she's always
spawning margins)

(will he ever find a
flavorless alley)

(but a tobacco **hiccup**
usually enhances the
pinprick's wake)

(never again will he
consider **peas** erotic)

(**magenta** does not exist in Geneva)

(redux)

(as if the number of **carats** is symbolic)

(although the audacity of the cruelty was not his primary **concern**)

(imagine **that** caravan of hags)

(actually, can waves be **gothic**?)

(expensive **bone**, that ivory)

(why wouldn't the sea **swallow** gold coins since they glint?)

(what is nullified when butter **melts**)

(though it is the hunted, coral **warns**)

(even **false** witches can samba)

(she's always bullish on the bogus, e.g. "knight or monk, **or** vice versa")

(cooks lacking **insurance**!)

('twas the **first** time she sewed for bit maps)

(dungeons: a waste of **marble**)

(regret a kingdom with **unknown** borders)

(she means, the **marrow** of obliquity)

(forgiveness become **brass** coin)

(snow **rents** the night sky to maximize the clarity of a flood losing its center)

(is it not impossible for a decade to **weep**?)

(oh, the awkwardness **of** trust!)

(she's always **spawning** margins)

(will he ever find a **flavorless** alley)

(but a tobacco **hiccup** usually enhances the pinprick's wake)

(never again will he consider **peas** erotic)

(**magenta** does not exist in Geneva)

IV

• • •

NEGATIVE SPACE

"Some time later, he came across a similar thought in one of Flaubert's letters to Louise Colet (August 1846) and was struck by the parallel: '...I always sense the future, the antithesis of everything is always before my eyes. I have never seen a child without thinking that it would grow old, nor a cradle without thinking of a grave. The sight of a naked woman makes me imagine her skeleton.'"
—from **The Invention of Solitude** *by Paul Auster*

82...

...Not so. Encounters are not like engravings, whether
on marble or wax, their images like words even if
everyone agreed on the definitions of texts. There will
be no code. You can never hear what you read...

83-84...

...Hiding places are inherently temporary. Delay
through prayers. Proceed through "the present
gruesome time" without delusion: to hide something
already hidden is a worse negation than mathematical
cancellation...

84-1...

...None of us are immune from desiring gratitude...

84-2...

...I want my lover to become immortal for, how else can I receive sympathy—if not praise—for my position as lamb?

84-3…

…Forgive how he honors her memory by bragging
about her metaphors…

84-4…

…Why must we terrorize dust…

95-1...

...To be human is to be anti-ghost, though many will fail
to concede this out of romance...

95-2...

...As a point of view, "we are all autistic, or none of us
are" engenders poems...bludgeoning poems...

95-3...

...Was it really sneering snow, or was it just a terrible day?

96-1...

...The creature defiled the umbilical cord noosed about its neck by opening eyes and naming the world with a scream...

96-2...

...The baby (I first typed "body") is trying to breathe
while the mother smokes a cigarette...

96-3...

...Does obsession preclude or facilitate note-taking viz
tiny words from cramped fingers?

96-4...

...What does it mean that I see a claw and want to kiss it?

96-5...

...Such an ardent student of the escape!

96-6...

...How to choose between moral vs financial hardship?

97...

A legacy comprised solely of an imperious state.
Ye angled beak!

98-1...

...Nostalgia defined by the concept of "shepherds and shepherdesses"...

98-2...

...The predictability of Apollo's jealousy...

98-3...

...Is it irony or something else that a mad woman bears children who grow up to be a Pope, a Sultan, and the Russian emperor...

123...

...Using touch to teach language...

124...

...The ease with which sleep masters...

125-1...

...Splintering wood as if the sea can escape itself...

125-2...

...Perhaps the sea is not a woman...

127...

...Chewing leaves for consolation, as if love is chemical...

128...

...English as a shipwreck...

131-1...

...The lack of irony in the carnivore being imprisoned
within walls of meat...

131-2…

…Kisses beginning a 200-page absence…

142-1…

…The painting's true gift is the peace of
contemplation…

142-2…

…Discordant when the artist's intention is reversed: red walls, then a floor of pale violet…

142-3…

…Certain colors inflict revenge…

142-4...

....Sketching the room one is not inhabiting...

143...

...The person diminishing before the passion s/he once engendered...

150-1...

...She enslaved empires through open-ended stories...

150-2...

...Fiction as a tool for forgiveness...

152-1...

...The jealousy of wives always bespeaks cows...

152-2...

...The gazelle become metaphor for companion when one attempts to obviate loss...

155-1…

…To reach maturity "with nothing in their eyes"…

155-2…

…No food…

155-3

…She cannot forgive herself for introducing another's face to nervous twitches…

155-4…

…Lust in loss…

157-1...

...To look at the sky and feel that even this cruelty will end...

157-2...

....Crying alone in an empty room, thus creating another empty room with which to fill the first empty room...

157-3...

...What causes a man to fast...

158-1...

...Blood surfacing from sidewalk cracks like violets heralding a change in temperature...

158-2…

…To rape is to lie…

161…

…Souls lost because they thought they can unfold all of eternity's folds

164...

...Living in daydreams, not as rehearsal for lives outside dreams...

171-1...

Proclaiming this text to be a conclusion, thus *making* it so...

171-2...

...Puppies never deserve their inevitable adolescences...

172...

...She understands that constantly reading how others die from weeping will not prevent such as her fate...

Forgotten Page...

...The sky will not be here again...the earth will not be here again..."where are you?"

V

X̶Y̶Z̶

COUPLET

~~My~~ Poem?
Your Call

SONG ~~IS SUBJECTIVE~~

the world ~~is never~~ unclad
~~confused as to whether lashes detract or~~ enhance<u>s</u> eyes formed
from ~~pale blue~~ sapphires

~~open window,~~ Bach…*faintly*
retrieving that thought ~~I didn't know was missing~~

~~asleep,~~ she beheld him then
(scent of a lunatic) ~~negative~~

rough ~~skin a~~ map
~~reproduce~~ half-tones from a photograph

what makes a language move ~~left to right on a page~~
~~O,~~ what crusade ~~is this?~~

~~her~~ gown extends ~~her~~ skin
~~a hug~~ picked by ~~small,~~ slanted bones

~~cry, because the~~ air is *felt*
~~stillness of the barn,~~ moss rising between slate ~~tiles~~

which ~~one~~ story ~~to retain?~~
~~the sunray~~ sears the stallion

then, intimacy as a glisten~~ing patch of skin~~
~~the~~ shutter steadies itself

~~feeling cheated at overhearing~~ one is a source of happiness
~~browning~~ edge of lace ~~forming narrative for "ancient"~~

~~metal~~ chocolate
~~oily~~ handshake

omission ~~as~~ confession

VI

?

SECRET SONG

The world unclad
enhances eyes
formed from sapphires

Bach...*faintly*
retrieving that thought

She beheld him then
(scent of a lunatic)

rough map
half-tones from a
photograph

What makes a language
move
what crusade

Gown extends skin
pricked by slanted bones

Air is *felt*
moss rising between slate

Which story
sears the stallion

Then, intimacy as a glisten
Shutter steadies itself

One is a source of
happiness
edge of lace

chocolate
handshake

Omission Confession

VII

THE PUNCTUATIONS SEND A POSTCARD

*Mixed Media (cut-up postcard from The Peninsula, a
New York City hotel; Singer brass snap fasteners, Scotch
tape; red and blue ink), 5 X 7" (2005)*

"THE SECRET LIVES OF PUNCTUATIONS"

Mixed Media (cut-up postcard from The Peninsula, a New York City hotel; Singer brass snap fasteners, Scotch tape; red and blue ink), 5 X 7" (2005)

I thought to create a postcard image that manifested the theme of this poetry collection, as articulated in its title *THE SECRET LIVES OF PUNCTUATIONS, VOL. I.*

I chose a postcard from a hotel because trysts, a form of secrets, can be held in hotels. I cut a strip from the bottom of the original card to size it at 5 X 7", one of the two sizes allowed for becoming part of the 2006 INTERNATIONAL HAND MADE POSTCARD EXHIBITION (IHMP Exhibition) in Kuala Lumpur, Malaysia.

I then divided the sliced-off strip into five portions, atop of which I wrote five punctuations addressed in my book: colon, semi-colon, parenthesis, question mark and ellipsis. I chose red ink to feature the punctuations as red is the color for passion…and lipstick.

Using a snap fastener, I pinned each of these symbolized punctuations to one of the hotel rooms of the hotel. There is a sixth snap-on fastener missing a punctuation, both to symbolize "secret" and to reference one of the punctuations not represented from my book: the strike-through.

I used snap fasteners to pin the punctuations against hotel rooms because these fasteners are usually used in clothing. So to unsnap or snap them references undressing and dressing—activities relevant to (secret) trysts.

I also used the snap fasteners in a reverse way; the back—not the front—of the fasteners are what's visible, again to reference secrets in that the "normal" public façade of the object has been subverted or masked.

In addition, I made visible the back components of the snap fastener because I actually found them more pleasing to the eye—which is to say, more appropriate from a formal (sculptural) point of view and to imply that the secrets of punctuations provide pleasure. The latter element is significant since the work refers to a poetry book and it is my ideal that poems give pleasure to their readers or viewers.

I wrote the title atop the postcard, then placed scotch tape across the title. I did so to prevent the ink from further bleeding, as well as to reference how the ink is now "masked" by tape. Of course the text is visible from beneath the mask/tape. The visibility of secrets relates to the revelations of which punctuation is unfolding its secret within which hotel room.

Those involved in secret hotel trysts rarely send out postcards about their acts. But because my poetry collection reveals "the secrets of punctuations," I also thought the postcard medium to be appropriate for it proclaims a message to the world. Specifically, even if a postcard is mailed to a specific recipient, the fact that its message is not hidden from postal service workers and others who may see it means that its message is "public."

Relatedly, I intend for my poems to be "postcards" to the entire universe.

152

VIII

A DE-OTHERED GAZE AT
"THE SECRET LIVES OF
PUNCTUATIONS"

The Secret Life of Punctuations

By Leny Mendoza Strobel

I never told the Roshi this: I have cheated during zazen
at the zendo. Instead of counting my breaths and
following the comings and goings of thoughts while
sitting, I stare at the wall in order to tease out a story
lurking within the veins of the wood's grain and the
gnarls in its nubs. I see an awe-struck eye. A creased
brow. An upturned lip. Sometimes there is a mirage that
invites an interpretation, a nudge in one's memory bank
of a forgotten story.

I am aware that there are rules to be mastered if one is to
attain the state of Emptiness. Yet something tells me that
I can bend the rules if only to see what lies behind the
disobedience. Emptiness can wait.

Punctuation marks remind me of this. The rules of
English grammar on punctuation are succinct, non-
negotiable. That is why my grade school teacher didn't
spare the rod in order to discipline us on their correct
usage. Over time we demonstrated perfect mimicry, ever
mindful of the dire consequences of a misplaced mark—
a red mark of failure or a slap on the wrist. We learned
our punctuation lessons well.

Now we rarely notice them except when they are mis-
used. Perhaps that is the point: One is never meant to
notice them and yet upon this invisibility a writer builds
an elegant sentence or a scaffold of ideas making reading
pleasurable. Pause here (,). This clause is independent of
the next (;). Exclude this []. This points to this (:). End
here(.) and so on…

For a postcolonial subject like me, the rules of English
usage didn't come in a vacuum. They came in nicely

packaged as a "gift" from the empire to its colonial outposts—so that what is unintelligible might become intelligible; what is obscure might become clear; what is dis-united can be united within one language. So much the better for management of the empire and its unruly colonies.

Time has been kind to the life of Punctuations. The rules are still more or less fixed and undaunted by the malevolent and mischievous tricks played by nativized englishers (non-native English speakers). Partly, it is their invisibility or lurking presence that do not invite grave attention from the grammar police.

Now comes *THE SECRET LIVES OF PUNCTUATIONS, VOL. I* by Eileen Tabios. What happens when a poet decides to foreground punctuation marks and gives them a life of their own? This poetry book is organized this way:

Semi-colons
Colons
Parentheses
Ellipses
Strikethroughs
Question Mark

The poems in **Semi-Colons** all begin with ";"—how do I, the reader, supply the preceding clause to complete the idea here—

> ; To Study Art Is To Become Thin

I have to admit, it is not easy! There isn't necessarily a narrative here about studying art or becoming thin. Yet there are images here that prefigures the feeling that comes with falling in love with Art.

; despite Cezanne's desire, the world is never
unclad
; to peruse a painting (intently) and see only
one's uncertainty over where to look
…
; white velvet ribbon become bookmark
; lace

I notice that the titles of the poems and the last line echo
back to each other, yet in between there are halves of a
thought/image/feeling, with the first half waiting to be
filled in by the reader.

; The Loss of a Wool Coat

; exodus *[last line]*

;The Possible Glow

; ember *[last line]*

; Hope for Enchantment

; bells *[last line]*

Two of the three parts to the section on **Colons** are "The
Estrus Gaze(s)" and "*from* The Masvikiru Quatrains";
the former is inspired by Autism and the question of
whether it is a disease or an identity and the latter by the
Shona sculptors of Zimbabwe. The poems in "The Estrus
Gaze(s)" hearken back to a time of "archaic darkness …
when all things were one," "a never ending pattern," a
"holograph" —perhaps as if to say that autism is not a
disease.

Eileen references the Shona sculptors of Zimbabwe in "*from* The Masvikiru Quatrains" for allowing the vision in their minds' eyes to emerge through stone effortlessly and delicately. She triangulates this with the work of another poet, Jukka-Pekka Kervinen, who generates poems via a computer program that "generates statistical distributions…to avoid patterns" and allowing a period "." when the computer encounters a space from the vocabulary source. The poet attempts to discover if this manner of constructing poems generate a musicality—a soundscape—with their own rhyme and rhythm and tone.

Eileen takes this process one step further: She strings together three-line words from Jukka's text and inserts a colon after the first word to create relationship between these words. Out of the abstract threesome pairings, I was surprised and bemused by these (there are many more but here's a sample):

> professor: minutia civil (The Eighth Page)
> mastermind: keynote whitener (The Ninth Page)
> gulag: floppy mandatory (The Eleventh Page)

The point of Eileen's poetics here, for me as a reader from a postcolonial space, is a type of de-familiarization with punctuations. The difficulty of responding to these poems lies in the forcible manner by which one must contend with the punctuations before one contends with the words.

The shorter chapters, **Parentheses, Ellipses, Strikethroughs, and Question Mark,** continue this refrain: what happens when we break the rules? What happens when we de-familiarize ourselves from the very things we take for granted like punctuation marks?

What happens when the ellided, marginalized and invisible take on center stage on the page?

As I write this, I am reading *Postcolonial Melancholia* by Paul Gilroy. He asks the same question but in a different but related context: How can we avoid recycling the narratives of an imperial past that has become useless to the present? How do we deal with the post-imperial trauma (of Britain and by extension, the U.S.) that must rely on these recycled narratives to keep the dead empire alive? How do we deal with the Other who now lives in the (dead) empire's center? How do we get rid of racism that is at the root of Other-ing?

His reply: De-familiarize the familiar. Dis-entangle ourselves from the old narratives. Withdraw our consent from the empire's attempt to continue fanning the fires of racism and xenophobia in the name of protecting the empire's image of its glorious past. Face the reality of the traumatic consequences of colonial conquests.

Could it be that one way of doing that is to begin to look at the greatest tool of the empire of the 19th and 20th century: the English language and its grammar rules?

In a way, I see Eileen de-familiarizing punctuations in these poems. In giving them new and not-so secret lives, she challenges the reader to conjure new relationships, new images, new stories. What was new and difficult for me in taking on these abstract poems is the musicality that wasn't easily evident at first glance. Perhaps that, too, is conditioned by my inherited sense of rhyme and rhythm coming from certain places (e.g. hip-hop, Cordillera rhythms, salsa) that doesn't include poetry. In this exercise, I needed and wanted to expand the boundaries of my experience of what is musical. In this sense, poetry has ceased to be an "Other" for me.

Thinking back to why I broke the rules of zazen, it occurs to me that perhaps I have simply become tired of obeying the rules. I ceased to believe the Roshi when he said that I must sit for another 20 years before I can experience Emptiness. In his view there is only one way. He didn't want to know where I had been—what other practice in my past might have offered me a glimpse of Emptiness -- he just wanted me to find his way. He is right, of course, and many believe him. But I was ready for what lies beyond the fence.

For those who are ready for this kind of wild and good ride, this is the book.

Leny Mendoza Strobel is Assistant Professor of American Multicultural Studies at Sonoma State University. Her latest book, a multi-genre collection of poems, prose and visual art, is A Book of Her Own: Words and Images to Honor the Babaylan *(Tiboli Press, San Francisco, 2005).*

IX

ABOUT THE COVER...AND MORE

The Punctuations Point to Eve Aschheim

At one point, while preparing this collection for publication, the Punctuations reminded me of Eve Aschheim's paintings because their imagery is deceptively minimalistic. That is, her gestures, to me, are spare and yet robustly active; her cover image "Conway" as well as "Lurker" on P. 163 draw the viewer into the works, in the same way I hope for my poems to draw in their readers. Despite their simple marks, Eve's paintings are also lushly evocative, such as "Not Not-White" on P. 166. When I considered her Artist's Statement about her "lines," it seemed fitting to heed the Punctuations' call to put one of her images on the cover of this book, as well as to invite her to share her paintings' presence within the book's contents. For when Eve says about her line paintings that they allow her "to explore dynamics of little lines, and their possibilities for creating space, implying virtual form, suggesting form, and activating the space through movement and tension", she well can be speaking about my own efforts in the Punctuation Poems. I'd written these poems partly to attempt using tiny details (punctuations) to robustly energize. This is but another way of saying: the poem begins the poetry experience but its recipient, the reader/viewer, completes it.

A goal, too, may be akin to how, as Eve puts it, "lines paradoxically become streaks of light."

—**Eileen Tabios**

"Lurker" 1999. Mixed media on duralene mylar,
12 X 9 in. Photograph by Farzad Owrang.

ARTIST STATEMENT

Investigations of different kinds of space have compelled me for many years. "Lurker" is an attempt to take a perspectival space and make it non-representational, or less representational, without gravity. "Conway" is an attempt to register hyperbolic space in Reimanian geometry, the geometry of curved surfaces (as described to me by Professor John Conway) .

My most recent works are the small line paintings, such as "Not-not white", which allow me to explore dynamics of little lines, and their possibilities for creating space, implying virtual form, suggesting form, and activating the space through movement and tension. I have been fascinated by how subtle marks create energies and affect, sometimes dramatically, the direction or meaning of the piece. The lines may suggest the movement of particles under the influence of various forces: gravity, wind, the geometric ordering of nature and the changing structures of thinking.

With a spare vocabulary I attempt to generate maximal effect so that the paintings add up to more than the sum of their parts. When I move one line slightly, the entire composition changes. Every line is a player in a complex and subtle web of relationships. Some marks are aligned with geometric structures, others float freely, while others hover at the intersection of various compositional systems, mediating the space between them, rendering these systems compatible while holding them in conflictual opposition.

In some of the paintings, the lines seem to form all-over fields; however on prolonged viewing, one realizes that multiple structures emerge. In some paintings, small lines torque the plane of the canvas. The lines can also be seen as the edges of objects or planes, the trajectories of objects in motion, or markers of space. In the layered space of the painting, some lines float behind the picture plane, while others are clearly on the surface of the canvas, and still others seem to be floating in the view's space.

Suspension, flotation, transformation and implied motion are key. The small lines are forms that can allude to sub-atomic particles, dust, rain, or wind-blown elements. I attempt to register the forces at work in both the visible and invisible world. In some paintings, the lines paradoxically become streaks of light.

—**Eve Aschheim**

"Not Not-White" 2003. Oil on canvas panel, 16 X 12 in.
Photograph by Farzad Owrang.

X

THE PUNCTUATIONS' POSTSCRIPT

SELECTED NOTES TO POEMS:

MY BAYBAYIN POEM
The poem was constructed partly based on a remix of two articles: "Old friend helps A's Sweep-up" by Susan Slusser, and "Fonda, Lopez romp through generation gap" by Mick LaSalle, both from the August 30, 2005 issue of the *San Francisco Chronicle*.

; SONG IS SUBJECTIVE
The poems were written while reading—and being inspired by—Siri Hustvedt's novels *What I Loved* (Henry Holt & Co., 2003) and *The Enchantment of Lily Dahl* (Henry Holt & Co., 1996).

OCTOBER 30, 2005
Each line's phrase before the double colons is quoted from Parts 6 and 7 of A.R. Ammons' long poem, *SPHERE: The Form of a Motion* (W.W. Norton, 1974).

THE COLON'S MIRROR: DOUBLE COLONS
These double-colon poems were featured in the author's poetics blog (http;//chatelaine-poet.blogspot.com), as follows:

THE CHATELAINE'S POETICS Blog
Tuesday, August 30, 2005

SERENDIPITY POETICS
Serendipity is as useful a muse as anything.

Belatedly, I've added a section of "double colons" to my manuscript that'll become my 2006 book, *The Secret Lives of Punctuations, Vol. I*. The process began when I read one of Barbara [J. Pulmano Reyes]'s poems which used two colons in between phrases. I initially thought she meant the punctuations to suggest the phrases can work backward and forward viz the colon-based relationship (if/then)—which is to say, I posited a narrative relationship. She didn't, though appreciated my read, but had meant it in an equally interesting manner, to wit—"a visual experience occurring with the double-colons, as if it means to give the reader space but also suffocate that space, in addition to their functioning to slow the pace down to a struggling crawl."

Sorta shades of Jose Garcia Villa with that attempt to use the punctuation to slow the pace of the poem (re his comma poems). Or P. Inman (with his period poems). [Or Alice Notley (with her quote makrs).]

Of course this got me started thinking more about double colons (being so focused as I am at the moment on punctuations)...and then I happened just hours ago to FINALLY read A.R. Ammons' 1974-published long poem *SPHERE: The Form of a Motion*. His use of the colon is simply brilliant.

SPHERE is perfect form—how the colon keeps the energy/momentum going so that the long poem never flags. To wit:

Perfect : : Form : : Perfect.

And so obviously how that circling back gets at the concept of a sphere. Again—just a brilliant conception by Ammons.

And all that led to two poems that will comprise my double colon section in my *Punctuations* book! Colons that question which phrase generated which conclusion. Actually, this also touches on a long-held poetic interest of mine—writing poems that can be read forward, backward, left to right or right to left...

Two poems, the first dedicated to Barbara and the second dedicated to Thomas Fink who'd suggested I check out Ammons' *SPHERE*.

Anyway, that whole process that led to my double-colon poems can be called serendipity. Or, to suggest again that when one is open to the world, the world rewards your attention with poems.

*****

169

UPDATE: A peep queried about an example of what I mean by poems "that can be read forward, backward, left to right or right to left..." There are examples in my book Reproductions of the Empty Flagpole, *a collection of prose poems. Several of the prose poems are comprised of paragraphs that, were you to reorder them (including reading them backward as they're presented), might still work. This effect would make sense given that one of the influences to those prose poems is cubism...so that narratively, they're not linear anyway and the referential juxtapositions can seem arbitrary....*

THE ESTRUS GAZE(S)

The poems were written in response to parts of *Songs of the Gorilla Nation: My Journey Through Autism* by Dawn Prince-Hughes (Harmony Books, 2004). "The Estrus Gaze" relates to, among gorillas, the female's signaling a desire to mate.

THE MASVIKIRU QUATRAINS

The series "The Masvikiru Quatrains" is dedicated to Jukka-Pekka Kervinen.

Of much help as regards Zimbabwe Shona Sculpture is *SPIRITS IN STONE: The New Face of African Art*, by Anthony and Laura Ponter (Ukuma Press, 1992).

Some of the poems were published by *maganda* magazine's issue on "Power, Choice and Change". The poems were sent to the *maganda* editors with this note:

> I wrote "The Masvikiru Quatrains" by practicing *maganda's* theme of "Power, Choice and Change." The words in these poems are lifted from the long prose poem "cornucopia" by Jukka-Pekka Kervinen. By stringing together three-line words based on my sense of poetic music, I amended *cornucopia*. By doing so, I thought to question whether my "power" over Kervinen's text was negatively wielded if the result was still the same poetic music that had caused him to write his own text. I also insert a colon after the first word, as if to create a colon/conclusion type of

relationship between the first word and the next two words. The power, then, resides with the reader in determining whether such a narrative relationship can exist (a la Gertrude Stein's mode that putting two seemingly unrelated words together nonetheless creates meaning because of the nature of words). Thus, whatever [colonizing] power I exercised in reconfiguring Kervinen's text is also something I gave up ultimately to the reader of these poems. The paradox of this process befits, in my view, the inherent paradox of Poetry's ephemerality.

The following is the source text for "The Fourth Page," the first poem in this series:

Page 4 from Jukka-Pekka Kervinen's *cornucopia*
foolery chore notoriety smirch resilience drip pollinate eyrie baptize hemlock colliery progress retinal runners-up kilowatt periscope impersonate wane. forger unceasing nimbus dowdy round-the-clock ménage penetrate rot disingenuous moonscape gabardine ugliness cornucopia pimple front office. Overweening proton munificence wheelbarrow airship lire scalene denouement batch. Vaseline nose dive. Unintentional trading post. Substation blowup freebie scalene gem gas damper promiscuous monotheistic specialize lubricate alluvial betterment bloat trick narcissi permissive conductive gritty VCR handyman positron persuasiveness statehouse midget manipulative recalcitrant phantasy mantel IQ programmable. Crabbed Ra farmhouse fallibility space-age namby-pamby exportation stony hula slake inflexibility least faintness. Spontaneity instrument snowsuit steppingstone all-purpose odometer housecleaning anytime trot crystallization lachrymal cheesecloth mummer slickneses profuse bigot timbre AM corpus defeatism ahem misfire diplomat idiomatic unintended treatment dogmatic rations periscope thrash patent medicine. Watt malt swindle quarry inhalator rummage sale. Dwelling copter augment politician disguise hobbyist paleness flake

171

paunch nontransferable converse sheaves epoxy.
Hayloft. Iodize self-controlled semen discrepancy
nerve gas. Trlllion speller deterrent bravery planetary
wintergreen veritable autonomous anthem
praiseworthy circle lumber jealousy digit leeway
advantage tortuous thimble commissar lachrymal
gainful pushiness reformatory protector lodge
slippery atty. Campanile Na voltmeter imprisonment
jewelry softball issuance Frequent small fry.
Quiescence liquefy. Chicken pos. downwards
Touching averse impassive amicable perquisite
truthfulness Postage nevermore proceeds levelheaded
groceries breaking and Entering. Copra markup
monastic viability nameless feasibility Clubhouse
eyeliner beast panorama negotiable dorm Pisces
Decadence announce tremendous outflank tweedy
browser Idealism offal viviparous conceal iterate
conjoin uncounted badge Jr. stay malcontent salary
boldfaced swordfish. Meek thermal Plainclothesman
radicalism dire thin-skinned capital punishment.
Baker's dozen. Skin southeastern detainment N. Mex.
Woodwind Upstart medicinal. Bunk assortment
gravestone outmaneuver Hungarian picture tube.
Pointy Mediterranean fend conclusive

PARENTHETICALS
The parentheticals were written initially via handwritten
reactions on each page of Jukka-Pekka Kervinen's collection,
obeyed dilemma (xPress(ed). In transcribing the poems into the
typed manuscript, I found that I couldn't read much of my
handwriting...so the published results are also secondary
parentheticals from the original parentheticals to Kervinen's
text.

NEGATIVE SPACE
All text result from responding to—and specifically attempting
to contradict—text adjacent to all ellipses in Paul Auster's
novel *The Invention of Solitude* (Penguin, 1982).

ACKNOWLEDGEMENTS

My thanks to the editors of the following publications
for featuring poems from this collection:

{1111} journal of literature & art (California College of the
        Arts) (Eds. Youmna Chlala & Brent Foster Jones,
        with thanks to Steffi Drewes & Peach Friedman
        for raising this opportunity)
Blue Fifth Review (Ed. Sam Rasnake)
Cutbank Poetry (Ed. Brandon Shimoda)
Eratio (Ed. Gregory Vincent St. Thomasino)
Famous Reporter (Ed. Ralph Wessman)
Hamilton Stone Review (Ed. Halvard Johnston)
Kwikstep (Ed. John Marshall)
Literary Well/Pozo Literario (Ed. Edwin Lozada)
Maganda (Eds. Kristina Ordanza and Vin Salvatore)
MIPOesias Revista Literaria (Guest Ed. Tom Beckett &
        Ed. Didi Menendez)
Moria Poetry (Ed. William Allegrezza)
Mystic Prophet (Ed. John Marshall)
New Zealand Electronic Poetry Center's FUGACITY
        0 5 Online Poetry Anthology (Eds. Brian
        Flaherty, Bernadette Hall, Claire Hero, Michele
        Leggott, Graham Lindsay & John Newton)
One Less: Collections (Eds. Nikki Widner & David
        Gardner)
OurOwnVoice (Ed. Reme Grefalda)
Shampoo (Ed. Del Ray Cross)
Sleeping Fish (Ed. Derek White)
SOFTBLOW (Ed. Cyril Wong)
Spore 2.1: Ekphrastic Writing (Ed. Crag Hill)
The Wandering Hermit Review (Ed. Steve Potter)

The poems in ": THE ESTRUS GAZE(S)" were published
as *Belladonna Chapbook #67* (Eds. Erica Kaufman & Rachel
Levitsky, Brooklyn, 2005).

Some poems from "The Masvikiru Quatrains" were published as an e-chapbook, *SONGS OF THE COLON*, by Ahadada Books (Eds. Jesse Glass & Daniel Sendecki, Toronto and Tokyo, 2005).

"(redux" was the September 2005 Featured Poem at Kundiman (www.kundiman.org), curated by Sarah Gambito and Joseph O. Legaspi.

The Afterword essay for, and some poems from, "The Masvikiru Quatrains" were published in *Moria Poetry* (Ed. William Allegrezza).

"; HOPE FOR ENCHANTMENT" was part of a "Poems Form/From The Six Directions" poetry-wedding performance during the October 8, 2005 wedding reception for Michelle Bautista and Rhett Pascual in the San Ramon Marriott, San Ramon, CA

The postcard-art "The Secret Lives of Punctuations" was exhibited at the *2006 INTERNATIONAL HAND MADE POSTCARD EXHIBITION* curated by Suzlee Ibrahim and Nalur Seni at the Garden of Art, in collaboration with ARTPROJECT2006, in Kuala Lumpur, Malaysia.

Much love was given this project throughout poetry blogland. Thanks specifically to Jean Vengua's *OKIR*; Rebecca Mabanglo-Mayor's *Bringing Wor(l)ds Together*; Rochita Cloenen Ruiz's *Raindancer's Map of Memories*; Michelle Bautista's *Gura*; and Tom *Beckett's Will To Exchange*. Thanks as well to Ivy Alvarez for kind words at *42 word review*.

Maraming Salamat to Leny M. Strobel whose courage has made her a poet's "Ideal Reader."

Thanks to Eve Aschheim for her receptivity to the project and participation in it.

As ever, Heartfelt Gratitude to Jukka-Pekka Kervinen whose own poetic brilliance makes him a poet's "Ideal Publisher."

A BLURB PROJECT:
The Secret Lives of Blank Lines

_____

_____

_____

_____

_____

_____

_____

— _____

Your Name Here

The blurb ideally should be written with each new (unmediated) reading of a poetry collection. Dear Reader, After engaging with this book, you are invited to share your "blurb" (positive and/or negative). Send by e-mail to GalateaTen@aol.com. The first 100 blurb participants will receive from xPress(ed) a copy of Eileen R. Tabios' previous xPress(ed) release, *MENAGE A TROIS WITH THE 21ST CENTURY* (2004).